I'm Determined To Be Somebody Someday

By
BARBARA SMITH-STERRETT

Copyright @2020 by Barbara Smith Sterrett

All rights reserved. No part of this book may be reproduced in any form or by any electronic or mechanical means, including information storage and retrieval systems, without permission in writing from the publisher, except by reviewers, who may quote brief passages in a review.

This publication contains the opinions and ideas of its author. It is intended to provide helpful and informative material on the subjects addressed in the publication. The author and publisher specifically disclaim all responsibility for any liability, loss or risk, personal or otherwise, which is incurred as a consequence, directly or indirectly, of the use and application of any of the contents of this book.

WORKBOOK PRESS LLC
187 E Warm Springs Rd,
Suite B285, Las Vegas, NV 89119, USA

Website:	https://workbookpress.com/
Hotline:	1-888-818-4856
Email:	admin@workbookpress.com

Ordering Information:
Quantity sales. Special discounts are available on quantity purchases by corporations, associations, and others. For details, contact the publisher at the address above.

Library of Congress Control Number: 2013923799
ISBN-13:   978-1-953839-13-8 (Paperback Version)
                           978-1-953839-14-5 (Digital Version)

REV. DATE:

Table of Contents

I'm Determined To Be Somebody 1

Be My Friend 2

Introduction 3

Dedication 4

Acknowledgements 5

Foreword 6

My Utopia 10

God I Need You 11

Being Chosen 12

I Have Been Looking 13

Chapter I
    Childhood 14

Chapter II
    My First Boyfriend 15

Chapter II
    Treated Different 18

Chapter IV
    A Vow I Made Michael, Vernell,
    and I Visit Nursing Homes 21

Chapter V
    The Ponderosa 30

Chapter VI
    Hurricane Katrina 37

Chapter VII
    My Ministry, Fourth Marriage,
    and Move to Louisiana 38

Chapter VIII
    Accolades to Mama on her 90th
    birthday August 20th, 2019 57

Chapter IX
    Accolades to Michael Dionn and
    Bobby Vernell Hookfin from your Mom 58

Chapter X
    My Move to Livermore, California 61

What Others Had to Say About Barbara (Babs) in
Livermore, California 63

Chapter XI
    I Tried 65

My Closing Remarks 71

About the Author 73

I'm Determined To Be Somebody

The present conditions and dark circumstances,
May make it appear that I have not a chance.
The odds may be against me, this fact I admit,
I haven't much to boast of – just a little faith and grit.
In spite of the things that stand in my way,
I'm determined to be somebody, someday.
There's no royal blood coursing through my veins;
No great family background for me remains.
My living conditions have been kinda bad,
But it makes no difference what folks think or say.
I'm determined to be somebody, someday.
Some may think I made a poor start,
Well, maybe I have, but I'll handle that part.
At the end of each round, I'll be on my feet,
For there's something in ME, that's hard to beat.
The fight may be tough, but I'm in it to stay,
For I'm just determined to be somebody, someday.
There's really somewhere that I would like to go,
There's truly some things that I would like to know,
There's certainly some things that I'd like to see,
And something special I'd like to be.
Let others do as they will or may,
But, as for ME, I've just got to be somebody, someday.
As a member of a once down-trodden race,
To the courts of Heaven, I've appealed my case.
I know that Jehovah is the judge on the bench.
Tho' man may deride, and lynch;
My blood will cry from the ground and say:
Tho' you slay me, I'll be somebody, someday.
My head may be bloody; and my skin may be black,
But nothing shall throw me off the track.
I'll climb the ladder round by round,
Until my feet strike higher ground.
And when I do, just remember what I say:
I'M DETERMINED TO BE SOMEBODY, SOMEDAY

Anonymous

Be My Friend

When you think I am wrong
Be my friend
When life has taken its toll on me and I feel alone
Be my friend
When there are decisions that I cannot make
Be my friend
When you see that I have lost faith; have understanding
Be my friend When there are tears that continue to flow
Be my friend When my enemies are encamped around me
Be my friend
When I utter my innermost secrets; keep them
Be my Friend

Barbara Smith Sterrett

Introduction

This book of my thoughts, poems and letters from m friends is written to inspire, encourage and challenge all who read my book. My hope is that you will learn from the many mistakes that I made and do not be afraid to make mistakes, for this is how we grow. Learn to follow your own mind and do not let others shame you into doing what they want you to do.

My vision is to let my light shine before others so others will see Jesus in my life.

To my soul mate, Ralph Owens, for his Love, Affection and Support when I needed him most during the writing of this book. To all my good friends, and foes I cannot name, may God continue to bless you!

Dedication

I dedicate this book to Jesus Christ who sacrificed His life for all, to my father, Jessie Lee Smith, Sr., Mrs. Willie Mae Fontenot, Mrs. Buena Freesia Tricia Ann Galloway Harrison (my fifth grade teacher), my grandmother, Bernice Demones, my Auntie Norma Murphy, Mother Dear (Hazel Lucas), Eddie Bell Harvey, Russell Brokenbough, and Charles A. Sterrett, Charles Jones, Mrs. Annette Floyd, Auntie Asalee Smith Vernon, Mr. and Mrs. Jesse Harvey, Aunt Frances Wilson, Joyce Elaine Moore (my older sister), Rev. Herbert Guice Jerry (Gerald) Smith (my younger brother), Mrs. Mary Ruth Woodson, Mrs. Sue Hudson, Uncle Billy Demones, Aunt Andean Quinn, Mrs. Alameda Hudson, Owen Daniels, Mrs. Mable Williams and Dolores Bennett who always encouraged me.

They are all deceased.

I dedicate this book to my mother, Mrs. Artis McGowan, who lives in Amite City, Louisiana for being my mother and my friend.

- My Goddaughter Nakia White
- My sons, Michael and Bobby Vernell Hookfin, for the strength they have given me over the years.
- My soulmate Ralph for his support and encouragement.
- All my good friends, and foes I cannot name, May God Continue to Bless You!!

Acknowledgement

I want to express my profound gratitude to:

- Mr. and Mrs. Tommy Williams for their support during my college years.
- My sons and their mates, Mike and Virginia, Bobby and Joniann. I am always their mother, always their friend and always stand for Christ in front of them.
- My father who was there when I needed him(deceased).

  My mother for giving me her inner strength.
- My baby sister, Lynette R., for being there for Mama as her other sibling works.
- My baby brother, John (Tree), and his wife LaShawn for their work in the ministries.
- My sister Karen who never let her love fade.
- My brother Larry for helping me with my handicap center in Oakland, California in 1975.
- My brother Jessie for taking good care of me as a little girl growing up and still looks out for me today.

Foreword

*1*950-2013: I, Barbara Ann Smith-Hookfin-Franklin-Stephen-Sterrett, have experienced being poor, a mother, divorcee, having two legs, one leg, a stroke, and a happy relationship. I was born 11 September 1950. On the 24th of May 1968, I graduated from JJ Gulledge Hawk High School in Tylertown, Mississippi. October 10, 1968, I was hit by a Southern Pacific Train in Watts, California. I received no compensation. On the 19th of February 1969, I married and became a mother on November 8, 1969. In March of 1972, my second son was born.

In July 1972, I found my first job since losing my limb. I worked for Internal Revenue Service. I left in 1975.

In 1975 I started a center for the handicapped, called Handicap Research Institute, in Oakland, California, and I took Dale Carnegie Public Speaking. I ran the handicapped center for two years. In 1977, I went to college full time. In 1981, I went to a concert in Fukuoka, Japan. Sponsored by the Fukuoka Sister City Society of Berkeley, California and the mayor of Oakland, California. In 1982, and 1983, I subbed at Amite High School in Amite, Louisiana. In 1984, I graduated with honors and received two scholarships from Merritt College in Oakland, California. In 1987, I graduated from California State Hayward in Hayward, California. I retired on SSI from the Internal Revenue Service (IRS) in San Francisco, California.

I remarried November 16th of 1996, and moved to Amite, Louisiana in February of 1998. On September 2nd of 2002, I had two mild strokes that left me in a wheelchair. In August 2005, I was a victim of Hurricane Katrina, and moved from Mississippi to Hayward, California in 2007. My happy marriage was over.

In 2008, a good friend of mine, Ralph, moved me to Sacramento, California, where I currently reside in a senior complex. I lived in Los Angeles twice in 1964 and returned again on my 18th birthday in September of 1968. In October of 1968, I was on my way to work at an Interior Decorating store, where I worked as a sales clerk, in Watts, California, when I was suddenly struck down by a Southern Pacific Train as I crossed the intersection at Long Beach and Vermont. This train, traveling at a speed of 30 miles per hour, hit me and dragged my body 30 feet, cut my right leg off, and my left thumb cut in half.

As a born-again Christian at the age of eleven, I was compelled to call on the name of Jesus as I lay on the train tracks bleeding, and in tremendous pain. I promised God that if he allowed me to live through this ordeal that I would be a witness for him with my family, as well as my friends.

God was so gracious to grant me my wish.

With what I know now, I realize that my trial was not Justice. I was classified as one of those kids who burned Watts. I lived near the coliseum, 4202 Dalton Avenue, Los Angeles, CA. My phone number was 213 291-8178. One of the men who worked for Southern Pacific Train Company said, "The train could STOP on a DIME." I felt within my heart that, based on all the evidence, the jury would be just. I was working during that time and going to college at night. I was not using drugs. There was no train horn blowing and there were no crossing bars at the intersection of Long Beach and Vermont.

The judge was a Criminal Judge, and this was his first Civil Case. He advised me not to show emotions that might influence the jury. I was obedient to his request. The jury consisted of twelve white people. One juror, in particular, was a mom with an eighteen-year-old daughter. During the jury selection, my attorney thought she would be an asset to my case, as I was only eighteen when this happened to me. I trusted God in my heart, I believed that the jury would do the right thing. I was looking forward to the jury granting me what I deserved which would give me security and pay for my education. Moreover, I had lost my job.

As a result of this accident I could no longer perform the duties of my job, which required me to walk and stand for long periods of time-sometimes all day. I am appalled to report that I was not awarded any compensation for this accident. This accident that changed my life forever.

Across the hall there was another Southern Pacific trial going on at the same time. The jurors were all white, the victim was a sixty-year-old white male. He had an accident with injuries that were no way as extensive as mine, and he did not lose a limb. He was awarded $100,000.00 for damages he suffered.

I asked myself where the justice in this is. This weighed heavily on my heart after I lost my case and learned of the compensation he had received. I thought of committing suicide. I stood on the roof of the courthouse leaning over on my crutches as I cried. I don't remember how long I had been there, but I heard a clear voice say, "It's a nice day," it was repeated three times. At that point I turned to my right, saw a bright light and an Angel with a Japanese face smiling. The voice said to me, "STOP, you are chosen, I have work for you to do," it was not until I went to Japan that I realized that the angel God had used to spare my life was Japanese.

In 1972, I was determined to find a job. Department stores, fast food chains and grocery stores all considered me a bad risk. It wasn't until I had called over twelve operators before the thirteenth operator went the extra mile and found a rehab center for me to call. It was through this center that I got a job at the Internal Revenue Service, where I worked for three years. My job was challenging, and I came home with sores and pain daily. My job again required a lot of standing, but I had a supervisor who was compassionate and understanding, she allowed me to take frequent breaks when needed. After working there two years, my supervisor retired, and a new supervisor came aboard. This supervisor was not as compassionate and understanding as the previous one. Due to the fact that I appreciated my independence and wanted to keep my job I never complained. So, during my third year of employment I resigned from the IRS and continued my education at the local Community College at night. The long distance across campus between classes presented a problem for me so I stopped going.

After leaving the IRS I founded the Handicap Research Institute in 1975. I accomplished this goal with a high school education and a limited community college education. Over the next twelve years I struggled through getting my AA degree. My struggle was because of my difficulty with walking and my bouts of depression.

It took me sixteen years to keep my promise to God. I returned to Amite, Louisiana where I worked as a substitute at Amite High School. I was determined to be independent. I attended Southeastern University where I worked on my degree three days per week. I also held down a part time job as a news reporter for the News Digest, as well as participated in my local church activities. During this period, I worked closely with my family and tried to initiate ways for us to develop a closer relationship and communicate better.

By now, I had two unsuccessful marriages. But as a result, I was blessed with two wonderful sons. Even though many in my family and friends looked at me as handicapped, I never grieved that loss. I was determined that others see me as the strong, complete person that I was. I worked overtime trying to accomplish this and prove them wrong. This was more than I could bear and resulted in me having a nervous breakdown. I ended up in a mental institution in Jackson, Louisiana for twelve days.

After I recovered from my breakdown, I had the opportunity to re-evaluate my promise to God regarding my efforts to reunite and communicate better with my family. I came to the conclusion that where I connected and obtained a successful relationship with my dad, I was not as fortunate with other members of my family. It appeared we had become further apart. I later decided to return to Oakland, California, where my sons lived. When I returned to Oakland my income consisted of SSI and grants. I attended school full time during the day. There kwere mobile carts to take me to and from classes, this was a great help. As my up and down bouts of depression continued, I decided to get a therapist and learned that I was borderline bipolar. I have been able to stay in balance with therapy and medication.

After graduation I returned to work for the IRS. I continued to work on my education and started to pursue my MA degree on the weekends. However, while working, my old physical concerns and challenges came back to haunt me. Again, I was in a lot of pain and had a great manager who was willing to work with me. This manager eventually transferred. By that time, I had about ten years invested in the IRS. Due to the stress, my goal of receiving my MA degree suffered, as I was unable to complete my thesis. However, with my determination I was not willing to give up, I had my doctor and therapist write letters requesting a different job that would allow more flexibility. This was not good enough. The manager suggested that I resign. An older co-worker overheard our conversation, he suggested that I read the Union Manual under Retirement. I learned that I could apply for disability retirement. I won!!!!! Thanks to another person who went the extra mile-he just happened to be white.

In 1977, I began to write poems and songs as therapy. I was one of four disabled people chosen through Merritt College, Fukuoka Society and the mayor of Oakland, California; I was fortunate in being chosen to sing at the International Handicap Concert. It was there I had the opportunity to sing one of my poems, "Everybody Needs Love." By 1987, my third marriage was over and I had retired from the IRS in 1994. I met and married for the fourth time, he was a retired Navy man who loved to keep busy. I felt so blessed to be married to a Christian man who loved me, spoiled me, and supported me physically as well as emotionally. We met in East Oakland Church of Christ, in Oakland, California, we seemed to click.

My Utopia

My Utopia can be reality
My Utopia can be reality
My Utopia can be reality
I have a vision
I must have a vision in life
Even if only I can see it, feel it
Taste it
I must follow my vision just like
Plato, Aristotle, and Locke
The difference is my vision has a
Solid foundation, an unmovable
Foundation, a reachable
Foundation (love, caring, sharing my vision)
Just like Apostle Paul, Prophetess Debra and
David
Any side can be under
Construction and the foundation
Will stand solid
With my vision, I can improve
With my vision I can reach out
And make a difference through
Love, caring, and sharing
Yes, my Utopia can become a
Reality because I have a vision
And I am following it each day

Barbara Smith Sterrett

God I Need You

Somewhere God I have lost faith
Somewhere God I have lost hope
Somewhere God I have lost courage
Dear God increase my wisdom
Dear God increase my knowledge
Dear God increase my understanding
Dear God I need you now

Barbara Smith Sterrett

Being Chosen

Being chosen by God one is put through many tests
People of all walks of life are watching us.
How do we carry ourselves?
How do we smile?
Do we offend easily?
Are we different?
Being chosen makes us different not better
Being chosen helps us treat others with kindness
Being chosen helps us to carry ourselves in a respectable manner.
Being chosen teaches us to wear a smile
Being chosen teaches us not to offend easily.
Being chosen puts us in the Royal Family Being
chosen by the world is what each of us desires,
but being Chosen by God is the Greatest of All

Barbara Smith Sterrett

I Have Been Looking

In All the Wrong Places
All I want is to be loved
All I want is to be held
All I want is to be happy
All I want is security
All I want is friends
All my wants have not come through
I have been looking to man for all my wants
I have been looking in the wrong places
Now I know God can give me
ALL my needs and some of my wants

Barbara Smith Sterrett

Chapter I

Childhood

My childhood home was located in Smith Hill, which is six miles east of Arcola, Louisiana. We lived in a wood frame house with a wooden stove in the kitchen, and a wooden heater in the living room. This home originally belonged to my grandparents on my father's side. My aunts and uncles lived in that very same home when I was small. I remember there being wallpaper on the walls and some areas had hole in the wall. One of the things I enjoyed most was singing on the porch (like today's patio) and waiting for my dad to come home, he would be drunk but sometimes he would bring us boil peanuts and crawfish,

Then he would accuse mama of other men's coming to the house while he was gone. She would try and defend herself by talking back and he would abuse her. I always prayed that he would go to sleep and not abuse mama verbally and physically. But it did not always work.

When people came to visit, my siblings and I were sent to the backyard to play. One of my cousins had five children and they would not come outside, they stayed in with the adults. They were spoiled brats. My cousin, who lives in Portland, Oregon and I laugh about it today. Gloria said I looked so homely.

I was the third child in the family, my older sister was raised by my grandmother. (my mother's mother) She was not my father's child. Mama said daddy was mean to her and would spank her for no reasons. That's why she let Big Mama raise her.

My siblings were as follows: Elaine, Jessie Jr, Jerry, Larry and me. 12 years later mama had a boy and two girls. I always believed that these three children gave mama extra strength to live. Elaine was killed in a car accident when she was 18th and Jerry died from a heart attack some years later in the woods. He was a logger like our dad.

I always found ways to get my brothers in trouble. Once I made Kool-Aide out of Mama's jam juice and gave it to them. I didn't realize that when I took out some of the juice, it left a ring in the bowl, so we all got a whipping.

Mama and Daddy had their bed in the living room, along with a sofa and a cast iron heater. I had my own room next to theirs with a private entrance from the front porch. The three boys all shared one room. I had to go through the boy's room to get to the kitchen. We had an out house, so at night, we used a bedpan. We also had a room for Big Mama, my mother's mom.

Growing up as a child can be rewarding and sometimes very difficult. Rewarding in that I learned how to farm and gather and eat what we grew. It was difficult, because being in the country, I had to get up at 5am to help mama prepare breadfast. My brothers would tease me and say the biscuits were hard as bricks.

My job everyday was to feed the chickens in the morning and gather the eggs in the evening. We had a small garden, if there was anything to be gathered before school, we had to gather it.

I had to wash dishes after supper (dinner today), I could not relax after I ate. I had to clean the kitchen, sweep the kitchen floor and the living room/bedroom floor. Daddy would be laying in the bed watching every stroke I made with the broom. He had his shoes in a certain spot and I had to move and sweep there and put them back in the same position. I made a vow that when I grew up that I would not wash dishes or sweep until I got good and ready.

My brothers had to feed the hogs as well as get the produce from the garden. My father was a logger, so he would keep my brothers out of school Monday thru Thursday to help him cut logs. On Fridays, the school would have tests. Because my brothers only came on Fridays, they would not pass the tests. They soon became discouraged and dropped out. The chores seemed to never end, we had to bring grass from the field to plant in the front yard. We had well water that we pulled up with a rope. It was very good water. We had to peel posts that was used to build fences. My brothers even had to cut wood for the stove and heater, my father would mark on the porch where the wood needed to be placed. To earn extra money my brothers would work for my great uncle gathering his crops. My father worked on Monday thru Thursday, and Friday thru Sunday he would spend at the bar room and with other women.

I was a sad child. My name Barbara and Smith meant to me, "Blessings are sent." I received clothes from my aunts in California and from my Mother's Day job. To me those were blessings. I had a secret place in the woods, where I would daydream. I would dream of me being on stage speaking words and people were listening to me. I don't remember what I was saying, but I was somebody very important. To this day, when I get lonely and sad, I go back to this vision and I see myself letting my light shine on stage being a leader and others would listen to me.

I went to school up until the fifth grade in the country. My mother was afraid of my father, so I did not get to go to my graduation. I cried all night. My eyes were swollen, but I took pictures in my cap and gown the next day.

I graduated to the sixth grade and went to school about 11 miles away. At that time, it was still an all Black school. Except for church, at school this was my first experience with an inside restroom.

Mr. AC Sims drove the bus. My cousin Lynn and I were his favorites. We gave him letters each week to mail to our boyfriends. We talked to cousins. They would send us 5.00 a week for school. There was a store we passed on the way to take other students' home. Mr. Sims would leave us at the store while he transported others home, he would come back to get us later. I was known as the country girl going to school in the city. I was the only one who never went to town on weekends. I was a grown woman before I went to town in the Amite, Louisiana.

I was not allowed to play sports or go to any games or go to any parades. Mama was afraid to let me go because my dad maybe abusive to her. We all took lunches to school; I took butter biscuits and jelly sandwiches. The other students had slices of bread and had ham, bologna and cheese sandwiches. I would hide behind behind a tree to eat because I was ashamed of my lunch. When I finish, I would go where they were.

Chapter II
My First Boyfriend

Eddy was my first boyfriend, he sought my dad's permission to date me, and I was 12 at the time. Since my dad was a logger Eddy had to go to the woods to speak to my father about dating me. My brothers often teased me about having Eddy as a boyfriend. They would say he is going to get you with a baby like he did the other two girls. He was 17th. I would meet Eddy at my secret place in the woods, this was the place where I daydreamed. Eddy was six feet tall and very handsome. At an early age I lost my virginity to Eddy because he promised to marry me. He always used protection and said we would not have children until I graduated from college. Since he was older, Eddy already had two children by two different girls, this is not what I wanted for me, this would have been too much for me to handle.

Many times, he asked me to run away with him, but I was afraid that he would abuse me verbally and physically. I was a stubborn person and always had to have the Last word.I knew Eddy cared for me deeply, but when it came to love, I was unfamiliar with that term because no one ever used the word love in my household. The closest thing to love was Eddy visiting me on the weekend and bringing me a loaf of bread, baloney, cheese, and a strawberry soda.

My father was very abusive to my mother. These episodes took place every three to six months. Once when we got off the school bus, mama would get out of the truck and daddy would get out and beat her all the way home. We would see pieces of her clothes where he had torned them off my mother's body. He broke several of her ribs and other parts of her body over the years. I would pray to God that my father would not kill my mother. It never entered my mind to pray for him to stop abusing her. These episodes affected me to the point that it made me so nervous I wet the bed every night Mama began getting me up at night to keep me from wetting the bed.

Doing my marriage, if I got into an argument and was upset and nervous, I would wet the bed. My grades in school suffered as a result of my dysfunctional family. My grades were C's and D's. There was a big difference in the experiences of city kids and kids from the country. City kids knew nothing about outside plumbing, farming, or chores that go along with being from the country. They had inside plumbing and their chores were consistent with chores inside the home using modern appliances.

At the age of 13, my dad gave me permission to go to California to continue my education. Two of my cousins were driving to Los Angeles and they were willing to take me with them. Eddy was unhappy about my decision to leave, but I was going anyway. Mama made me fried chicken, biscuits, and jelly sandwiches. During the ride I daydreamed a lot about being someone very important. I was thinking no more outside bathroom, no more picking beans and strawberries, no more chickens to feed or gathering eggs, and most of all, no more nervous stomach. The countryside was beautiful, and the ride through Texas appeared to take forever. After driving day and night for two days, we finally arrived in California.

My great aunt whose name was Connie, had two daughters named Norma and Hazel. I called them Auntie Norma and Mother Dear. I stayed with Mother Dear, who had a son that was five years younger than me. I did not have a suitcase when I left Louisiana. My clothes were packed in boxes. My great aunt made this statement, "You can take the Nigger out of the country, but you can't take the country out of them." I could feel my stomach becoming nervous again. She did not give me a chance to relax. She had me in the backyard raking leaves while her grandson sat watching TV.

I heard from other relatives that my great aunt was very hard on family members from the South. These are a few chores that were assigned to me: washing dishes, washing clothes, ironing and cleaning the house. These chores I did while her grandson watched TV. He was spoiled.

Whenever we went to the movies, he always got the most money. I didn't understand why there was a difference made if we were all family. I made a vow, that if I ever had children, I would not make a difference. It reminded me of when I had to beg my dad for lunch money and my brothers refused to ask him. It seems that I had left one pain and came into another kind of pain, but I was determined to be that person in my vision. I vowed I would never give up.

It was a culture shock for me at the new school in Los Angeles, California, so many different races of people. It was refreshing not seeing "Colored," and "Whites Only," written on doors. I continued to write to Eddy, but I also talked to other boys at school. I got lost going to school every day, and my great aunt would not let me leave with the school kids early. The school had combination lockers and I was not used to them. Someone had to open my locker every day. My grades improved but I still had a nervous stomach and wet the bed.

I enjoyed living in Los Angeles, but I did not like my great aunt's attitude towards me. Whenever she would talk about my mother, I had a habit of rolling my eyes in a mean way. My great aunt would say, "I gave your dad six dollars to marry your mother legally and he gave it back to me. Your mom should have left him." I did not know that my mother and dad were not legally married. Their marriage was considered common law because they had been together more than seven years.

When I rolled my eyes at her she would threaten me to say, "I will send you home any time I get ready."

My great aunt's daughter and son in law worked at night and slept until 3:00pm the next day. By the time, her grandson and I got home from school, his parents would be up, and dinner was served. My job was to make the sweet tea and gather the mint from outside to put in it. We discussed what we learned in school that day and that's how it was day in and day out.

After school was out, my aunt's would take a trip to Louisiana, Georgia, and several other states for vacation. Louisiana was our first stop to visit my mom. Mom wanted me to spend more time with her, but my fear was that if I did my aunt would leave and I would not go back to California with her. My aunt promised me that she would send for me. The day I was supposed to leave on Greyhound, my great aunt called my dad and told him not to send me. My heart was broken. So, for the 10th and 11th grades I attended school in Louisiana. Eddy had graduated from high school and was living and working New Orleans. He received a draft notice from the army, and I begged him to marry me so I could live with his relatives and finish school. He said no I would have to wait for him.

Chapter III
Treat Different

My father treated me as if I had a disease. He had my mama buy me my own wash pan and potty-chair. My chores were given back to me again, and all had been done before going to school. I began to go back to my secret place in the woods to remember my vision. I will never give up; I was always saying to myself.

I told my mom that if I didn't get a chance to go to my junior and senior prom I was going to run away from home. I didn't mean it, because I didn't know where I would go. My older sister had been killed in a car accident the year before. My father took me to the prom in his log truck (like a big rig truck). All the kids laughed at me, but I didn't care I was at the prom.

I went to school at West Side High until the 11th grade. It was the last week of school and we had a substitute teacher. He was six feet tall, black hair and brown skin. I was infatuated with him. I told him about my boyfriend being overseas and that he could bring things back for very little money. The substitute teacher asked if my friend could bring him back some suits. The next thing I knew I had agreed to meet him at his mother's house. I had on a pair of shorts, tank top, and flip flops. It was the Saturday before Easter. Aunt Eva, my dad's aunt had just fixed my hair (she made home brew and was very noisy). We kissed and hugged. Suddenly I realized I had been gone too long. The teacher began to walk back toward my home and my mother saw him kiss me. She yelled, "Barbara Ann come here and bring whoever that is with you."

I knew that if I went back home, I would be a prisoner for life. So, when the teacher began to run, I ran with him to his car. We drove around a white neighborhood for hours trying to decide what to do. The substitute teacher wanted to go and explain to my father, but I told him my father would shoot him and me.

All I could think about was why this had happened to me. I must finish high school, then I thought of my grandmother, my mother's mom, and she didn't like my father. I thought she lived hundreds of miles away, but she only lived 25 miles away in a town called Franklinton. I remembered how to get there because of houses and trees and stores we passed. I did not let him take me all the way to her house because I needed to tell her what had happened.

I jumped out of the car and ran down a dirt road and began yelling, "Big Mama, Big Mama." She came to the door saying where is your mother? I told Big Mama I have to finish high school.

Big Mama and I went to town to pay some bills and we saw her son Billy. "Uncle," I pleaded with him to take me to Tylertown, Mississippi with him and let me finish high school there. "My father said if we ever ran away from home do not come back," so I knew he would not come looking for me.

My uncle introduced me to his girlfriend and told her I wanted to go to school in Tylertown. Dean had a daughter five years younger than me, she said I had to obey her just like her daughter obeyed her. She wanted me to write my mother a letter to let her know where I was. It took three months and Dean made me write the letter. I wrote a sassy letter telling Mama I ran away from home and I did not have a baby, I just wanted to finish high school.

Dean worked at a cleaners and people would leave clothes over nine days and that's where I got my school clothes from the beginning. I wrote my aunt in Los Angeles, California and told her where I was and she called my father, he told her not to help me. She told him I was still going to school, and not pregnant, she was going to help me. She sent me clothes and every month she sent me lunch money.

Eddy was home from the Army visiting, he found my uncle and aunt's house. Eddy gave me his class ring from high school and promised to marry me when he got out of the service. This was on a Monday evening and on the following Friday he promised to bring me back an engagement ring (but he never showed), I never heard from him again.

I kept going home to see my mother on the weekends when my father was gone. It was getting close to time for me to graduate and I was very happy. I was proud of myself. My stomach wasn't nervous, and I wasn't wetting the bed.

Two weeks before school was over my uncle began to act up. He lost his job and started drinking heavily and abusing my aunt. I overheard him telling my aunt that he wanted to take me back to my father's house. I decided that I had to run away again because my goal was to finish school.

I ran away to live with a friend in town. She was an only child and had a very nice mother. My friend dated a teacher. She told me that I should date older guys too. My uncle had borrowed $28.00 from me and didn't pay me back. That was $28.00 meant for my class ring money. So, I did like my friend Linda said, I began to talk to this older guy and I asked him for $28.00. I told him I was a virgin and he respected that.

On one of the trips home to see my mother he came along. We stopped at the club between Mississippi and Louisiana, I leaned over to speak to a guy that I knew. The next thing I knew I was being slapped across the face. I suddenly remembered what my father had told me, have your own money and buy your own drink when you go out. I gave Buddy, the guy I spoke to, my phone number and marched outside. My date was behind me and took my class ring. The next day he gave me the ring back and said after I graduated if I was in town, he was going to rape me. I left town. During the time I stayed with Linda, I drank less liquid so I wouldn't wet the bed, but I still had nervous stomach. Linda lied to her mother about where we went.

The principal of the school I attended was a minister, and he didn't allow proms at the school. I started a walkout, and the minister let us have the prom. We also took a trip to Texas. My grandmother came to my graduation and I graduated with honors.

After graduation I went to Meridian, Mississippi for the summer. When summer school ended, my aunt asked me if I wanted to come back to Los Angeles, California. I told my aunt yes, I wanted to come back to California. My mother had had three more children by this time I was 17 years old.

The young man I met in Mississippi at the club, met me at the Greyhound bus station. We danced to the song, Stay in my Corner, by The Dells. Buddy is his name. He was a football star in Louisiana high school. His nickname was "foot Work." Buddy was going to Springfield, Ohio to live. My father never gave my mother an engagement ring. I wanted to be sure that I got one. I never heard from Eddy again. Bud and I kept in touch.

I got a job at an interior-decorator store, where I met Russ. He was an interior decorator. We began to date. Buddy decided to send me an engagement ring for my birthday, September 11, 1968, I turned 18. I accepted the ring. On October 10, 1968, I was very happy, I had no nervous stomach I did not wet the bed. My name meant to me "Blessings are sent." I walked to the bus stop and caught the bus to Vermont Avenue and Long Beach Blvd. I got off the bus at Long Beach Blvd. There was a train stopped on my right.

I began to cross Long Beach with other people. I was in a daze, and the last person crossing the street. Suddenly I was like a spider being caught up in a web. The train struck me and drug me 30 feet. People began to crowd around saying that I lived down the street. I had to tell them my name and phone number. I prayed to God that if he spared my life, I would go home and be an example for my brothers. A young man from the train came and made a tourniquet and pressed against my legs to stop the bleeding. I was taken to one of the best-known orthopedic hospitals in the area. The doctor did not think I was going to live. He said if there were any relatives to send for them, my aunt sent for my mother to come out.

While she was visiting me, my brother Jerry cut his two legs almost off with the power saw working in the woods with my father, Mama had to go back to Louisiana.

Auntie Norma sent for Buddy to come out to the hospital. About this time Buddy had joined the Air Force. The wedding was not supposed to be for another year. Russ told me I should not get married because Buddy was not the right man for me. By this time my whole life had changed, what was I going to do?

Would anyone want me now with just one leg? How was I going to take care of myself? Russ whom I met earlier, had leukemia and felt he could not take care of me properly. Maybe Buddy will make a career out of service and I could convince him to get married earlier than we had planned. Thoughts that stayed on my mind left me with the determination to survive and I was sure I did not want to go back to Louisiana. Eddy my first boyfriend called as soon as he heard the news about my leg being cut off. He still wanted to marry me – but in Louisiana. I was sure that was one place I did not want to be because I had a fear of being abused.

While in the hospital I met a woman, whose husband was having surgery, she bought me some make up and encouraged me to speak to a lawyer. Little did I know that my great aunt was planning to send me back to Louisiana but I got out of the hospital a day earlier which happened to be Christmas Eve.

After I solicited the support of a lawyer it was interesting to find out about the changes that had been made. By the time my lawyer got to the scene of the accident, the track suddenly had bars across it. As my lawyer came aboard, we learned that the jury was already chosen. It was an all-white jury. We were supportive of one of the jurors because she had a young daughter who was 18, my lawyer thought she would be an asset to me because of this.

My attorney wanted the jury to see the scar tissue on my stump so I was escorted to judge's chambers, where he advised me not to show any emotions that might affect the jury. I did as he instructed me.

Bud, who was my husband by then, wanted to do one thing with the settlement money and I wanted to do something else. He wanted to pay off bills and I wanted us to buy a duplex. We later learned to my bitter disappointment, that I had lost the case.

After hearing the news that I had lost the case, I went to the top of the courthouse and looked down. I thought of leaping over, when a voice to my right said, "It's a nice day isn't it." The voice said it again and then I heard it a third time. I turned to my right and saw a bright light and heard a voice say, "You are chosen, I have work for you to do." This brought me back to my childhood vision – my name Barbara Ann Smith Hookfin meant to me, "Blessings are Sent Home". How soon I did not know.

Buddy and I settled in Lompoc, California. It was there that I gave birth to our first son Michael who was born on November 8th, 1969. Buddy would only take me to church and the Laundromat. He proved himself to be faithful to members of his family and they came out to stay with us, which made matters worse for our marriage suffered. I felt as if I was an outsider in my own home. Every three months I went to L.A. to visit my aunt. I was not allowed to take the baby. This went on for at least seven years. We later moved to Oakland, California.

I was very disappointed that Buddy left my car in Lompoc – I hated him for a whole year. By this time my second son, Bobby Vernell was born. We called him Vernell. I agreed to the name because he promised he would sign papers to have my tubes tied. Vernell was six months old and we were still living in Oakland and Buddy was seeking employment in San Francisco, which I was not happy about, so he settled for a position in Hayward as a janitor for Macy's department store at night. He would not leave me any money or the keys to the car. Buddy and I divorced in 1986.

I was baptized at 11 years old and church was always important to me.

I prayed that God would not let anything happen to Eddy before I had the opportunity to thank him for all his help while we were dating. For three months I consistently had a dream that would wake me up during the night. The dream was clear, I could see someone being beaten but I could not identify the face. I often called home to check on my brothers and my father. My mom assured me they were all fine. Finally, I called my mom to tell her about this dream I kept having and she said, "Barbara Ann, Eddy is dead. He was robbed and beaten to death in New Orleans, I didn't want to tell you." I screamed and suddenly there was a knock at the door, it was 3:00am, I looked at the door and a smiling face came through the door saying, "I forgive you," and then the face that belonged to Eddy left. I wanted to attend the funeral, but Auntie Norma said that it was all over and there was nothing I could do. For three months I fought with Bud to let me go home to Louisiana to see my family and take the boys. Buddy was not in agreement. So, I did not go.

Chapter IV

A Vow I Made Michael, Vernell, and I Visit Nursing Homes

After Eddy's death I made a vow to the Lord that if he lay it on my heart to go somewhere and I could not explain why I had to go, I would go anyway. One of the times when Eddy and I spoke, he expressed to me that he was involved with a woman that was the mother of his two children and she wanted him to marry her. He told her that I was the only woman he would marry. I replied to him and her very smart like on the phone and said, "I don't want him." Soon after that conversation, Eddy heard that I had married in 1969, he later married after that.

That was the reason he forgave me. Whenever I would go home to Louisiana, I would always have contact with his mom and let her know I was coming to town so she could let him know. He once told my mom that if he ever saw me again, I would not go back to California. I went home every year until the day he died.

I stayed married to Buddy for seven years. I stayed in the house until we sold it. Big Mama came down to baby-sit the boys until she got homesick and went home three months later. The boy's begged her not to leave and she said she was going to come back. Vernell said Big Mama you ain't never coming back. We were living at 5600 E 16th Street in Oakland, California we stayed there until we sold the house. She was founded dead six months later by the postal person.

I was very talented with my sewing. I sewed for the boys as well as myself. At work my co-workers and the Branch Chief all complimented me on my clothes.

During that same time, I had divorce Buddy and I went to an attorney to see if I could reopen my case against Southern Pacific Railroad. I learned that I had exceeded the Statute of Limitations by three months, to reopen my case for losing my leg.

I was sad but, glad I didn't get any money especially if I could not use it for what I wanted. I wanted to purchase some apartments and Buddy want to pay bills.

One evening the boys and I drove around looking for a church. Buddy was Church of Christ and I was Baptist. In Lompoc he went to a Baptist church, but when we moved to Oakland he wanted to return to his original denomination.

We drove around East Oakland and we ended up on 20th Ave. and East 21st Street where there was a little church sitting on the corner. This was a Wednesday night, we parked the car and went in. Upon entering the church, the pastor, Brother Bob Lewis, his wife Sister Alice, Mother Jensen (Sister Alice's mom), and their three girls were praying for God to send some children and we walked in.

As the boys grew up, they were very protective of me. If someone stared at my limb, they would say, "Don't stare at my mom. Just ask and she will tell you what happened to her leg." The boys and I went to nursing homes together, read scripture, and sang songs.

I bought Michael his first car, I taught both Michael and Vernell how to drive. I checked out videos from the library on taking care of your car. They taught us how to check the oil, water, and the air weight in your tires among other things. When they learned to drive, they drove with their left foot. The instructor at DMV told them they had to learn to drive with their right foot. They explained that their mom only had one leg and she drove with her left foot. I assisted the boys in opening their first savings accounts.

Michael got his first job in the East Oakland Mall at 16. Vernell was 13 when he got his first job at his friend's father's hot dog stand. It was my goal to make men of these boys and teach them to be responsible and dependable. They are just that.

We were the first members of the church. The church began to grow. We began to have shut-in (pray all weekend) at the church. I met a woman at the park, her name was Destiny and she had two girls.

Destiny's children were the same age as my sons Michael and Vernell. It appeared I met Destiny just in time, she was a musician, and the church was looking for one. Brother Bob had his two brothers join the church, one was married and an alcoholic, and the other one had a good job and was single. At another shut-in service we learned the holy dance and I was able to balance myself without falling on my prosthesis. Destiny and the unmarried brother had been talking for some time and they announced their engagement. During a shut-in Sister Alice said Destiny was possessed by a demon. The unmarried brother called off the marriage. About a month later Mother Jensen had her niece come out to Oakland and he married her.

I learned that as long as it wasn't one of their family members doing wrong, Brother Bob would preach about it or if you were on the poor side of the family like the alcoholic brother.

Chapter V

The Ponderosa

Joel and I had the opportunity to buy a fixer-upper house that we called the Ponderosa in 1981 on 64th and Harmon Avenue in Oakland, California . There was a carriage house in the back and another house on the property. There was an artichoke plant that made me know that we should have this home because I loved artichoke. This was an omen to me. Our credit was bad, so he went to his mother and asked her to loan us the money. She decided to put her name only on the deed. When we fixed the house up enough to get a loan to buy it, we asked her to take her name off and put our names on it so we could get the loan to pay her off. (she refused to do so).

I was running the handicap center with money from my unemployment check. Joel was constantly losing money for lack of business from New York Life Insurance Company. The center provided jobs, took clients to the hospital, provided fresh vegetables one day per week. There were arts and crafts for stroke victims. My center was run by people in training from other centers.

My first grant was from Catholic Charities out of Washington D.C. Once I got the grant, I called my mother and told her to tell my three brothers that I could give one of them a job whichever one wanted to come. She said Larry had asked for my phone number so she would tell him first. I sent him the money to fly here.

We bought a van and a portable lift; Larry became my driver for the center. He learned his way all around Oakland. We needed more funds to continue to operate. I learned that the city had funds available. So I applied for a grant from Oakland. We got the grant, but some employee turned my brother in because he was a relative. This was call nepotism. He had to quit working for the center. He was my right hand, but he soon got a job working for Shasta Soda Company in Hayward, California

The building we were in was a good location, the owner offered to sell the building to me, I went to the city and applied for a grant, but they turned me down. I was already using my unemployment check to help carry the load and now my brother Larry was gone. I hired two grant writers and paid them out of my unemployment check. No grants were found. I only had enough in the bank to pay the taxes for my employees. I invited channel seven news to come out to do an interview. I asked all the people that we had helped to come out and do an interview-no one showed up.

So, I prayed about the situation and God gave me this message. Close the center, you cannot save the world. Go back to college and get your education. I left the center to two people who said that they would try to get the grant money to run the center. What they did do was spend the money that I had for taxes. Joel and I had to make that good. My stomach got nervous again and I began to wet the bed.

I decided to sell life insurance along with Joel and go to college in the evening. My first job I sold more policies than he did. Joel was a sore loser. I noticed that he only had females as clients. When I stopped selling to be his secretary, I knew that every month the bank account was short because he was taking the young ladies out to lunch.

Joel treated the boys like they were his. Joel was very good to them and they liked him a lot. Even though I let Buddy have custody, the boys came to visit every weekend. My auntie Norma said on her deathbed, "Let Buddy have the boys – they will love you more." I didn't understand but I knew they would be taken care of. I now know what she meant, trained them.

Joel's mother, Mrs. Frankhun and I raised chickens in the chicken house, and we had a garden that had greens, tomatoes, strawberries, corn and cucumbers. I sold brown eggs on campus. I was known as the egg lady. By now Joel had no income coming in. Once you sell a policy you get paid the whole year, but if that policy is dropped the money is taken back from your check. We were on the fifth year of our marriage when Mrs. Frankhun asked me why I was going to college she said, "You will never catch up." I told her I can always try to improve myself.

I began to feel the urge to go home. I could not explain it to my sons. I told them to pray about it. I asked Joel to keep my visitation and have the boys call me when they came over. He agreed. I went home, got into church and became a missionary and spoke at many places. I started taking college classes at Southeastern University in Hammond, Louisiana.

One of the daily newspapers was the News Digest. While looking through it I saw an ad for a clerical position. I told Mama that I was going to apply for it. She said it was a white company and no black people bought their papers. I went to the News Digest and applied for the position. The owner's name was Harold Griffin. He said you are not from around, here are you? I told him my family lives here, but I am from California and he asked me to be a news reporter. I covered city council meetings, basketball, baseball, and football games. I also did human-interest stories. Many blacks began to buy the paper and Mr. Griffin doubled his sales.

With a high school education, you could be a substitute teacher. I began to substitute at the high school in Amite, Louisiana. The students respected me, and the teachers made sure I had enough days to work. My two sisters told Mama to make sure I did not call on them in class. I told Mama I was their sister at home and their teacher at school. My sisters Ruth and Karen did not like me very much, but they saw the students at school liked me they began to like me also.

During this time, I still hadn't had a chance to grieve the loss of my limb. At home I was known as the one who felt she knew everything. I began dating a married man. My baby brother John was a basketball star and I gave him good coverage in the paper every time he played. His nickname was Tree, he was 6'7" and my dad was 6'4" tall.

I had many deadlines to meet and I wasn't getting enough rest or eating properly. My body broke down and I had a nervous breakdown. During this time my mother's brother died – he lived in another state. Mama had to go see about arrangements for her brother. Mama and Daddy had me locked up in Jackson, Louisiana mental institute. I spent 12 days in the hospital.

When I got out of the hospital, they sent me home with many pills, lithium was one of them and it made me look like a zombie. I moved around slowly. I was living back with my mother. My eyes had a glaze over them. I decided that I wasn't going to take medication anymore.

A nurse came out to see me and said I had something wrong with my brain. I wanted to know if they could cut it out. I was diagnosed as a manic depressive. She said you will have to take medication for the rest of your life. I started not taking the medication. My mom found meds in the toilet, by this time I was back to my normal state. One of my friends told me I could get on Social Security, but my mom refused to take me down to apply. My friend's father took me. I had my first check go to News Digest for fear that if it came home, I would not get it. I felt the urge to go back to Oakland, California to be near my sons.

Mama did not want to see me leave, but I made all the arrangements and went anyway. I transferred my Social Security to California and I began to see the boys on my visitation again, and I thanked Joel for seeing after the boys while I was gone. My thorn had subsided, no nervous stomach or wetting the bed.

I got a job at Peralta Administration Office in Oakland, California. I worked for two people and they were nice to me. I was their secretary. In 1983, I was an extra in a movie with Carol Burnett and Alan Arkin in downtown Oakland. I worked at Peralta about a year then I resigned to go to college full time. I was still driving the 1968 Ford that I received from the Department of Rehab. It took me 12 years to get two AA degrees. I received one in Business Administration and one in Community Services. I received two awards from Merritt College. I was chosen to go to Fukuoka Japan along with three young men to sing in concert, honoring the International Year of the Disabled in 1984. We sang one song in Japanese and I sang a song entitled "Everybody Needs Love Sometime," it was recorded live on a TV show for housewives.

I continued to go to church and take Michael and Vernell to Sunday school. I taught the adult class once a month. I was in the Mission class that would go to convalescent hospitals, I would even teach there. Mr. and Mrs. Tommy Williams adopted me and the boys, and church nights they would put money on the third Psalm page in my bible. This would help me take the boys out to eat and go bowling. They helped me until I received my BA degree. Bethel Baptist Church is where I and the Williams' went to church. Reverend Herbert Guice was the pastor. The church gave scholarships every year to anyone who went to college. I received a $200.00 scholarship every quarter. They supported me with an extra $200.00 to keep my 1968 Ford going while I was going to college. There were other members that helped me also.

I had a breakdown and had to go to a shelter, and manic-depressive became bi-polar disorder. They kept me for 72 hours and started me on more medication and made a suggestion that I should get therapy. So, I found a therapist that took Medicare and saw her once every month while I was in College. One of the things she told me was that I trusted men too much. She said watch what they do and not what they say. That helped me a lot. I received my BS degree in Sociology and Social Services with a minor in Sign Language.

In the student union there was a bulletin board with job announcements. There was a job announcement for the Internal Revenue Service, start now as a GS 7 if you have a BA Degree.

That wasn't my field but I had worked with them before, so I filled out the application. Upon entering the interview, I noticed that the person doing the interview was someone I knew, well I didn't know her personally, but I am sure I had seen her around the IRS environment. Her name was Linda, she went and found my old work history and I started work doing training making the same amount of money as some of my co-workers that had more years in. This took place in 1987.

I had a girlfriend named Celestine and I went by her house one Saturday morning. I got the telephone book and began calling car lots, telling them how much I made, how much I could afford to put down on a car and how much my note needed to be. One company said I have your car sitting on the lot you can come on down and get it; this lot was located in Hayward, California. Celestine took me out to the car lot and the car had 12 miles on it. It was a 1988 blue Hyundai. I kept this car for 12 years.

My name Barbara Ann Smith Hookfin Franklin Stephens meant to me, "Blessings are sent here for security." By this time, I had my third husband. I had divorced the first two and the third one was a minister, so I thought this was the right marriage. We had a small church wedding. My sons tried to tell me not to marry him because he had too many problems. I couldn't see it. They were ever so right. My thorn came back. He had a problem that goes deeper than the paper could hold. I moved out after three months.

He would take me to different Baptist churches, and he pointed out the male ministers who were gay, he would drive me around the Bay Area showing me gay bath-houses I tried to tell him God honored marriage. He filed for divorce. I was back in my old apartment. My manager Mrs. Wilson knew him from San Francisco and began to tell me all about his family. I met him through his sister, who I met in the Disable Student Center. His church home was in San Francisco. He was a probation officer and a foster parent.

I continued to work at the Internal Revenue Service. The job was very stressful. I continued to have pain and sores on my stump. I would take my prosthesis off at work and leave it in the smoke room. I would use crutches during the day at work. Co-workers who smoked began to complain so I couldn't leave it there anymore.

I had medical insurance with Kaiser Hospital, so I got a therapist there that I saw once every three months. My supervisor was very understanding when I had to get off the phone and go take medication for pain in my leg. She was transferred out of the unit and I got a new supervisor – he was not understanding. By now I had 10 years of service with the IRS.

I applied for other positions with the Internal Revenue Service but was always turned down. I wore a vest with a lot of buttons on them that had positive sayings on them. I was known as the button lady always with a smile. The branch Chief did not like my old supervisor and they said that I was the teacher's pet. I was not good at answering questions off the top of my head. It was very stressful for me and caused me to have more phantom pain.

I had more years than my new supervisor and his answer was if you can't perform then quit the job. So, I went to my therapist and I took all of the applications that I had filled out trying to transfer to a desk job and was turned down. I went to the union and they advised me that I could apply for disability because he had not reasonably accommodated me – I filed for disability retirement and won.

I was living in an apartment as a manager for free rent. I met many new people. I was still in the church. I was dating several guys; it seems like it took 12 guys to make one good man. There were two young men that I was interested in Ralph and Dub. Ralph worked for AT&T, and Dub was a security guard. I wanted to settle down and be a wife. Dub and I married in 1996. Three months later he changed. The marriage was basically over, but I tried t make it work. We argued everyday. I had to have the last words. Dub have a son and sister that was gay. He began to act as if he was gay. He sat with the same young man at church and they began to date and spent time together at the time we separated.

In public, he treated me like a queen. When we got home, he was Dr, Jekyn and Mr. Hyde. I thought my marriage would work because I married Christian mes. I tried marrying one that didn't drink, this was my first husband, but he was both verbal and physical abusivise. We stayed married 7 years.

My second marriage he drank, but he was not an alcoholic, he had a B A degree, but he would not use it. I negotiated a deal to purchased a house around the corner from my first house. The address was 5720 E. 16th street. We lived there. We stayed married 5 years. He was a good man and he loved my sons, I had very little patience because he would not get a steady job. Later I learned he remarried and used his degree to become a school teacher in Berkeley, California.

Dub ask me to file for a divorce, because he had met a "partner" and wanted to remarry. All I ask him was to keep me on his medical. He said he would. I could have gotten alimony and stayed on his medical insurance when I file for the divorce, but I didn't want to take advantage of him, so I trusted him. I wanted to be fair. As soon as the divorce was finalized, he took me off his medical insurance. I trusted God to provide for me the money to pay for my medical and he did.

Chapter VI
Hurricane Katrina

We were in Hurricane season once again. This was August 2005. Hurricane Katrina came along, and we lost everything we had except the car and items we brought along. We went to Amite, Louisiana to ride out Katrina. We stayed with my aunt Ora Bell. All the hotels were full.

We had a full tank of gas when we came to Amite. We were driving back to Biloxi to see the extent of the damage to our apartment. There was no gas being sold in Amite. Bathroom items were in the kitchen, kitchen items were in the bedroom. Sewer was all in the house. The mattresses and couch were wet. I became sick and we had to sleep in the car until morning. I asked my husband, "What are we going to do?" He said we will try to make it back to your aunt's home. I looked at the gas needle again and he assured me that we had enough gas to make it. My stomach was nervous, and we had to find a place of business where I could use the restroom.

All the way from Amite to Biloxi trees were down. We saw neighbors cutting them up and getting them out of the street so traffic could keep moving. In 2004, Vernell's wife sent for Dub and me to come to California for a visit. Now this happen. I call the boys and they said to come back to California and not to worry.

My name Barbara Ann Smith-Hookfin-Franklin-Stephen-Sterrett meant to me Blessing are sent home for security soon. I didn't know how soon. We drove to the Texas State line on a little gas. It was hot but we were afraid to run the air condition for fear of using up the little gas we had. My son Michael was on the internet locating a gas station that we could stop at once we hit the state line. Thank God for cell phones.

Chapter VII

My Ministry, Fourth Marriage, and Move to Louisiana

I was ordained as a minister in 1975, in San Francisco. I was assistant pastor in Berkeley, California. I didn't like the way the lady pastor treated her husband. She was very disrespectful. So I left there and went to another church in California. Ralph videotaped me bringing the message. This was a Baptist Church. Ralph could not make a decision to date just one girl, and I didn't want to be number two. Dub went to Church of Christ and they didn't believe in women ministers. We dated for about three months. I did not want to live in sin, so I felt we should get married. I felt we were adult enough to know by now what each of us wanted in marriage. I talked it over with the boys, and again they cautioned me. I told them that they were living their lives and I wanted to be needed too. The warned me that I did not know enough about him. I didn't listen.

Dub's pastor refused to marry us because I would not let him baptize me. So we went to Reno and got married. The first month we were together I knew the marriage was not going to work. He was a very private person. Ralph told me that it wasn't going to work. Ralph owned a rental property and I rented an apartment from him.

I felt if we moved back to Louisiana, our marriage would have a chance and I could get closer to my mother and father. We moved to Louisiana in 1998, and stayed with my mother until we found a place to rent. We lived in a mobile park for four months. Someone introduced us to Al Alack, realtor. We negotiated a deal to buy a house in Hammond, Louisiana.

The Churches of Christ in Louisiana were white. My brother pastored a Baptist church in Arcola, Louisiana. Dub did not want to go to it. We went to the white Church of Christ. We were the only black members. We were treated like part of the family. John (my brother) worked at the courthouse, many members knew him as Tree.

Dub decided that he did not want to be married anymore so he moved out of the house. He had had an affair with a lady and by this time my 1998 Hyundai had fallen apart so we traded it for another car. He took the car with him. I shopped and bought a car. During this time Dub was gone and I contacted Ralph and his plan was to send for me.

Before that happened Dub came back owing two car notes. They were trying to repossess the car. The boys sent me money to keep me going, Ralph sent me money.

Dub wanted a bigger house with two bathrooms. Al had a four bedroom house in Amite, Louisiana. It was a family street and we were strangers there. Dub didn't want my family to come by. He had gotten closer to my father in the beginning. We made sure my father had a color TV in the living room and his bedroom. We made sure he had a cell phone.

After Hurricane Katrina, Michael and Virginia, and Vernell (Bobby) and his wife Joniann and their friends told us to come to Hayward, California, and they would take care of everything. As we traveled back to California, Interstate 10 and Highway 55 were flooded, so we took Highway 20 all the way to California. I read the bible out loud while Dub drove the car. He drove all the way. We stopped along the way at restaurants and hotels they were very good to us. I wrote songs, poems and sentences to keep me motivated as we drove.

After the hurricane we went back to Biloxi to see the extent of damage to our apartment. It looked like the apartment had been a washing machine, everything was everywhere. Dub said he saw dead bodies in the water. Gasoline was limited. We had a full tank of gas when we arrived at Aunt Ora Bell's house in Amite, also we had to use lawn mower oil to get back to Aunt Ora Bell's house. She's my daddy sister.

We drove from Louisiana state line to Mississippi state line on a quarter of a tank of gas. My son Michael was on the internet searching for gas and told us where to get off. We did not turn the air conditioner on for fear of using gas.

When we made it to Hayward, California the boys and their wives, and all their friends had bought us new clothing and enough to outfit a one bedroom apartment.

There were family pictures on the TV. They took good care of us. They found us an apartment in Fair Oaks, California. Dub did not want to stay there. He heard they were giving away houses to Katrina victims in Yuba City, California. That didn't happen so we found an apartment and moved in. It was two hours from the boys. My sons did not get a good feeling from Dub, they felt that he was moving me away from them.

I had no time for my vision although it was still in my mind. I had always wanted to write a book since my accident, but never felt that I had accomplished enough to write a story. We had received a small business administration loan (SBA) for the loss of our property and personal items we had lost in Katrina. We became debt free and I had enough money to write my book.

As long as I stayed in the house and had no friends Dub was okay with the marriage. I began to volunteer for Red Cross and received a Hero Award. He began to say he didn't want to be married anymore, so I took the book money to rent me an apartment in Yuba City, California. We shared the car and we divided the furniture. We continued to go to the same church. We went in the same car, instead of sitting with me as usual he sat with a young man at the church, and they began to spend a lot of time together. I joined a mental health group that met every week. This gave me the courage to move on my own. I contacted Ralph and he began to drive up to see me from Oakland.

There was a senior complex being built in Dublin, California and they did not ask questions regarding the last three years. I put in an application for this apartment, it was in between the boys' houses. This was also close to Ralph's house. Ralph loved beer when he got off from work, he would drink beer and forget the arrangement he and I had made and he would not call. This would make me angry and I wanted to work on my marriage.

Dub had moved to North Carolina, I begin to call him and talk about getting back together. I just did not want to be alone, I wanted to share my life with a mate. I talked to the boys again about our discussion and they said, "Mama, he needs your income," why was I blind and could not see this. I felt I was wasting my time with Ralph and I could be spending this time on my marriage. My thorns was back.

I flew to North Carolina to visit Dub, and no one at the church knew he was married. The church had planned a seminar and I suggested that we attend. Every night after the seminar we had an argument. We graduated from the seminar and one week later Dub said he was moving out. I told him to go tell the deacons that he was moving out. He told the deacon that he didn't mind being married, but he couldn't live with me anymore.

I had a nervous breakdown again and had to go back to the hospital. He had bought a new truck, so I packed the old car with some of my clothes and I began to drive. I was not on a freeway. It was like I was on a Frontage Road, the road that runs along beside the freeway. I saw beautiful trees, cows, horses, pigs, chickens, and goats as I drove along. It was like I was on a sightseeing trip. I stopped along the side of the road and threw away jewelry and clothing. It was as if I were trying to run away. I drove until I saw a Bank of America and the Radisson Hotel nearby. This was the same chain hotel my sons put me up in when I come to visit them. Michael was going to send me to another institution and I didn't want to go. I took control of my life and I called Dub to come and get me. I went to the store one day and when I came home the insurance man was there. Dub was trying to have me locked away in a long term mental hospital, where he could take control of my income. The insurance man said, "I thought you said she had agreed to this," and he left. Michael and Vernell refused to come help me drive back to California. I had to call Ralph to come and get me. The Helen Street Church of Christ and the Livermore Church of Christ paid for the rental truck. Ralph and I drove the rental truck and pulled the car on a trailer from North Carolina to Louisiana.

Junior did not have a ramp for my wheelchair and there was so many bugs. After Ralph left for California I got depressed again and wanted to end my life. Junior talked to Michael and my son told him to take me to a clinic.

I was able to walk on one prosthesis some after the stroke. I was in the clinic in Hammond for 15 days. I met a nice young lady named Reese, we both smoked. My friend from California named Betty lived in Baton Rouge and she came to see me often. Betty bought me clothes, hairbrush and other items I needed. My worker found a group home for me in Marksville, Louisiana. I had to go up four stairs twice a day and attend school every day. The group home could not accommodate my wheelchair, it was too big, and I had to leave it at school. While I was in the group home I met Raymond. Raymond liked me a lot, he was very helpful to me every day. I told Raymond that I was talking to Ralph, who lived in California. Ralph came down to visit me and he said when the program was over that he was coming to get me.

I graduated from the program December 15, 2007. I did not want to stay at the program. Once we had a fire drill and everyone met outside and left me in my wheelchair on the porch. They laughed and said Barbara got burned up. This upset me and made my stomach nervous and I wet the bed during my stay there.

I graduated and Reese said I could stay with her and her husband but I felt I was in their way. Reese slept during the day and was up all night. I was very grateful that she allowed me to stay until January 28th when Ralph came down to get me.

Mama and I had not been speaking to each other, so for Thanksgiving she invited me to dinner. Since that time we have been talking to each other every day and night, sometimes twice a day and I was very grateful for that. I love my mother very much. She is precious to me. I love our phone calls twice a day, 8 in the morning and 7 in the evening, California time.

Ralph wrote several letters to me while I was Reese's house. Things he warned me to think about and try to explain to him if I could. Ralph is not a talker, he doesn't like the radio on while driving and it really has to be hot for him to put the air conditioner on. He looks at me in a way to let me know that he's very happy to have me with him.

I found an apartment in Sacramento, California. It's six years later and I am still here. We are older now, and decided that I could be number one in his life. At the clubhouse, where I live, I am on the activities committee. I help recommend different activities for the month. The activity committee is no longer active and there are fewer things for the seniors to do.

I started a Crochet, Knitting and Sewing Club that meets on Saturday mornings from 11:00am to 2:00pm, and Game Night that meets every third Saturday night of the month from 6:00 to 9:00. We have a 93 year old woman who is the Champ of Dominoes. We have tournaments and give prizes. Every Friday afternoon we play BINGO from 2:00 to 4:00.

Every Saturday our senior housing community receives bread from Safeway Stores, one of the local grocery store chains. This project is headed by Ms. Robbie. We are lucky to have her, she also makes all of our raffle baskets. On many occasions I read a poem or sing a song I wrote. You would enjoy them. Writing poems and singing songs help me to stay positive and I love encouraging people. I call myself a Motivational Counselor.

Ralph lives 90 miles away and he comes up every weekend. He takes me to my support group and to church. He does my washing and mopping the floors and shopping. He can make a mean breakfast, and great steak and potatoes. I can say that I'm really spoiled, but I like every minute of it.

We go out to eat, go to movies, go sightseeing and I go fishing in areas that I can use my wheelchair. Ralph does not like to argue and that's good. He likes to drink wine now and then, but when he gets sleepy he goes to bed. This is one reason I like living 90 miles away, he can't drink until he is at my house. Ralph tells me things would be different because he's retired. He says if I was closer he would be learning how to cook more.

In my life there have been three men who chose me and two are deceased. Eddy Bell Havier, from 10 miles east of Arcola, Louisiana, Russ Brokenbou, from Compton, California and Ralph Bernard Owens from Oakland, California.

September 2013, one night while I was working on my book, I had real bad phantom pains in my stumps. I accidentally took an overdose of pain pills. Ralph went back to Oakland, so he called to see how I was doing. When he could not reach me, he called my next door neighbor (Patsy) who had a key to my apartment. She called me and when she could not reach me, she called Robbie one of my friends in the apartment to come over. Patsy was also in a wheelchair. Robbie found me barely awake, so she call 911. The Doctor said I was very fortunate to get to the hospital in time. I finish my book December 30th 2013 and it was published January 2th, 2014.

I have known Ralph for over twenty-five years. I believe he is my soul mate from heaven. Amen, Amen, Amen!!!!

Katrina Prayer

Tonight, we are gathered together to Fellowship with one another

Red Cross; Board Members, Staff, Red Cross Supporters; Volunteers, Guests and Katrina Survivors as one Family.

As Katrina Survivors, this is our FIRST Christmas Holiday (not by choice) away from HOME, as we knew it. We appreciate all of you for being an extended Family to us.

We ask a SPECIAL BLESSING for those who are still displaced because of Hurricane Katrina and Rita.

We ask a SPECIAL Blessing over the food we are about to partake. Bless those who prepare it.

For whosoever shall give you a cup of water to drink in my name, YE BELONG TO CHRIST,

VERILY I SAY UNTO YOU, he shall not lose his reward. Mark 9:41

This we ask in Jesus Christ name. Let us say Amen.

Barbara Smith Sterrett

We're Survivors

1. Just the two of us-D&B Sterrett
Just the two of us-D&B Sterrett Verse:
We survive Hurricane Charlie, Ivan, and Katrina
2. Just the two of us-D&B Sterrett
Just the two of us-D&B Sterrett Verse: We have twin Angels, Grace and Mercy
3. Just the two of us-D&B Sterrett
Just the two of us-D&B Sterrett
Verse: Things happen for a reason You just believe
4. Just the two of us D&B Sterrett
The two of us-D&B SterrettJust the two of us D&B Sterrett
Verse: We survive Hurricane Charlie, Ivan, and Katrina
5. Just the two of us
D&B Sterrett he two of us-D&B Sterrett
Just the two of us D&B Sterrett
Verse: We have twin Angels, Grace and Mercy
Watching over us.
6. Just the two of us-D&B Sterrett
The two of us-D&B SterrettJust the two of us-D&B Sterrett
Verse: Things happen for a reason
You just believe.
7. Just the two of us-D&B Sterrett
The two of us-D&B Sterrett
Just the two of us-D&B Sterrett
Verse: You just believe –
just the two of us D&B Sterrett

Barbara Smith Sterrett

Interview with David Sloane, Special Projects on Take 5, Comcast TV

About Hurricane Katrina

Dub and I did an interview with Take Five Television in Yuba City on Comcast TV, with David Sloane. When the hurricane hit we were at my aunt's house. We were safe, but when we went back to Biloxi, to our home, that's when we ran into electronics, washer, dryer, clothing, everything was ruined. We left a day early so we would not be stuck in traffic. We went about 70 miles north of New Orleans to the town of Amite City, Louisiana. Normally when we went to my aunt's house we weren't affected by the hurricane. This time a tree fell in the roadway and the power had gone out. Aunt Ora Bell's house was soaked, Water came in under the doors, and through the bags of sand around the house.

Enough for a Lifetime

By Marty Evans, President and CEO of the American Red Cross
November 8, 2005

Imagine driving from New York to Chicago, 12 ½ hours for example, and seeing every neighbor getting help from each other. In 2004 a hurricane had hit. In 2005, When Hurricane Katrina hit, we helped 15 times as many people than in 2004. Please help your local Red Cross by donating money, time, and effort.

American Red Cross Hero Award Goes to Barbara Smith Sterrett

Guy Morrell-Stinson, "We made progress by coming from South Africa to America. The interesting thing is that Barbara Smith Sterrett is a member of the Church of Christ and had just come out of Hurricane Katrina, where she had lost everything and was willing to help us get furniture. This is someone had lost a limb and everything in Katrina and was willing to say we have enough, we want to bless you. We had not seen such generosity not even in our country."

Book of the Old Testaments

Genesis	II Chronicles	Hosea
Exodus	Ezra	Joel
Leviticus	Nehemiah	Obadiah
Deuteronomy	Job	Jonah
Joshua	The Psalms	Micah
Judges	Proverbs	Nahum
Ruth	Ecclesiastes	Habakkuk
I Samuel	Song of Solomon	Habakkuk
II Samuel	Jeremiah	Zechariah
I Kings	Lamentations	Malachi
II Kings	Ezekiel	
I Chronicles	Daniel	

Book of the New Testaments

Matthew	Ephesians	I Peter
Mark	Philippians	II Peter
Luke	Colossians	I John
John	I Thessalonians	II John
The Acts	II Thessalonians	III John
Epistle to the Romans	I Timothy	Jude
I Corinthians	II Timothy	Revelation
II Corinthians	Titus	
Galatians	Epistle of James	

The Names of God

-Hebrew Names-

- Elohim-Master; Creator; His Sovereignty (Gen.1:1; Deut.5:28; Isa.54:5; Jer.32:27; Ps.68:7)
- Jehovah; "My Lord God" (Gen.4:3; Ex.4:3)
- El Shaddai- "God Almighty," God's loving supply and comfort; and His power as the almighty one. (Gen.17:1, 28:3,35:11; Ps.91:1,2)
- Adonai-The Lord My Master, Owner (Gen.18:2, 40:11;Sam.1:15; Josh.5:14)
- Jehovah Rophe-Jehovah heals (Ex.17:15)
- Jehovah Nissi-The Lord My Banner (Ex.17:15)
- Jehovah Mikkadech-The Lord My Sanctifier (Ex.31:3)
- Jehovah Tsidkenu-The Lord Our Righteousness (Jer.23:6)
- Jehovah Shalon-The Lord is Peace (Jude 6:24)
- Jehovah Rohi-The Lord My Shepherd (Ps.23:1)
- Jehovah Shammah-The Lord is There (Ezek.48:35)
- Jehovah Jireh-The Lord Will Provide (Gen.22:14)

Resources That Help Me

- The Holy Bible (NIV), by International Society
- Explore Your Bible 2010, by Barbour Publishing, Inc.
- Hidden in His Hands, by Basilea Schlink
- NLT THE BIBLE PROMISE BOOK for Women, by Amy E. Mason
- Bible Promises for Women, by B & H Publishing Group 2003
- Promises from God's Word, by World Publishing, Inc.
- SKY HIGH FAITH, by Ken Gaub
- The New How to Study Your Bible, by Kay Arthur, David Arthur, and Pete De Lacy
- The Colors of Life, by The International Library of Poetry

News Digest

July 26, 1984

A Letter from California

By Barbara Smith Franklin

I was home in Amite from September of 82 until September of 83. While I was home, I attended Southeastern University, where I enjoyed it and met a great many friends and instructors. I also enjoyed the Baptist student union.

I was writing for The News Digest, part time, doing missionary work, attending school, as well as trying to cope with family crisis in my life. On my days off from Southeastern, I substituted at Amite High and it was known that the principal, Mr. Wayne, other faculty and students alike admired me and I them very much.

I feel that because of the overload in my life (unbalance) and my burning desire to be the best of all, it caused me to become sick the last few months of school and my family for many reasons felt the need to commit me to East Louisiana State Hospital (ELSH) in March of 83. I am not upset, nor do I have any regrets about being there. I was at ELSH only for a short while twelve days to be exact. It was apparent to me that I was overexerting myself and my life was not in a balance stage. My experience at ELSH was a rewarding and spiritual one, as I had a chance to sing and speak at the chapel there. I stayed in the Evangeline Hall. My desire is to return and do missionary work there.

My only regrets if any was having gone to the Hammond Mental Health Center and being assigned a counselor who could not relate to me. The counselor told my mother that I was using drugs and had the doctor prescribe a strong tranquilizer, which left me with very little control of myself. The pills caused me to act, look and feel like a robot and I could not see how to read without reading glasses. When I spoke to the head doctor about the counselor, he would not listen to me. I stopped taking that mind destroyer (Laxitane 25 mg) and began to pray. I soon came back to my normal self. Praise God! I told the counselor that I would not see her again and to assign me another counselor, preferable a male. By the time the assignment was made, September 26, 1983, I had returned to California and I have not taken any medicine since. God will and can perform many, many miracles in our lives if we let him.

I feel that by my returning home after being away for fifteen years, brought me closer to my father, mother, brothers and sisters. A vision that I had had for a long time and God allowed it to come past, while my parents were yet alive. I love them both dearly. I feel that the "lack of communication" is destroying many families today and I want to make a difference, while the blood is still running in my body, in my family. Hosea 4;6a says "My people are destroyed for lack of Knowledge."

When I returned to Oakland on September 17, 1983, I was in time to register, so I picked up where I left off in Junior College and graduated June 13, 1984. I received my AA in Community Social Services. I graduated with honors. I received the Human Service Award, The Student of the Year Award and was nominated for the Chancellor's Trophy Award all from Merritt College of Oakland. I also received the Merritt Chapter, Council on Black American Affairs Scholarship for $200.00 (MCCBAA) and was one of many members to receive the Bethel Missionary Baptist Church Scholarship for $200.00.

I was the recipient of these awards and scholarships because others saw and recognized my dedication through my volunteer work on campus and in the community as well as my church.

I was and still am a volunteer as a Let's Rap program at McChesney Junior High. The Let's Rap program is held during lunch time two days a week for students, who wish to form their own group, and have open discussion in a safe space. The school last year had thirty-four groups with the Let's Rap Volunteer Leaders coming from many different professions. While attending Merritt, I was a volunteer counselor in the Disabled Student Center. I was and still am a volunteer crisis counselor for a Community Women Center in Oakland. This is a 24-hour hot line for troubled women. I am able to work from my home through an answering service. A ten week training program was required before working on the hot line. I take at least two shifts a week. All of my volunteer work goes hand in hand with my major.

I will be going to California State University in Hayward, California, which is about fifteen miles from Oakland. I have put together a "special major" called Rehabilitation Counseling and Administration. I will minor in Sign Language. I not only want to work in a profession after graduation, but I want to keep the job too.

Because of my disability (being an amputee), I qualified for State Rehabilitation services and while I was in Amite, Dot Marten, a Rehab counselor in Hammond, worked with me to set up a program where I could receive my BA in two years. In September of 83, as I forstated, I made a decision to move back to Oakland, for many reasons. One being that I have two sons and I wanted to be closer to them. Ms. Marten, forwarded my academic program to my counselor in Oakland, however, the Oakland Rehab office will not honor the plan. Pass my AA degree. I refused to be defeated and I am in the process of filing an appeal. I also applied for a Pell grant and a Guaranteed Student Loan (GSL) of which I will received both and will be starting school as planned on September 27, 1984. It has been in the pass difficult for me to hold down a full-time job as well as go to school full-time and do my internship (volunteer work), so I am hoping to do freelance and some feature articles to give me some extra money for school.

Mr. A.C. Sims of Roseland is visiting his daughter, Gloria Sims Gilbert and his sister Anna Bell Sims of Jackson of Newark and Berkeley, California. He was asking to see me and my brother Larry. I went to see him on Monday, September 10th for two and a half hours. We enjoyed talking about old times. He said he was enjoying our town and weather. For many who do not know, Mr. A.C. was my school bus driver when I lived out cross the river, where my daddy still lives.

I am celebrating my 34th birthday today, September 11th while I am writing this article. My desire is to be financially independent at age 35. In closing, I would like to share two of my many favored scriptures from the Bible (KJV), II Timothy 1:7 and I John 4:4. II Timothy says "For God hath not given us the spirit of fear: but of power, and love, and of sound mind". I John 4:4 says "Ye are of God little children and have overcome them: because greater is he that is in you than he that is in the world."

I still do missionary work and volunteer work leading toward my major, but the key for me was learning when to say No, and taking out some time for myself to relax. I swim also for relaxation and this weekend September 14-16, I will be going with Gloria Sims Gilbert on a Christian retreat in Clearlake, CA.

I would like to again thank all of you friends and foes alike for all while I was home. I still receive The News Digest, phone calls and a few letters from many of you and I appreciate all of them. If you wish to write or call me, I would be glad to hear from you and I will respond. My address and phone is below:

Missionary Barbara Franklin
c/o Michael Hookfin
P.O. Box 43068
Oakland, CA 94624
(415) 534-5241

One Leg is Enough

If you cannot help me be successful
On one leg
Please do not stand in my way
Cause I am on my way to the finish line
One leg and all
Get out of my way
Cause you cannot stop me from the finish line
For I am on my way to success
With the greatest helper of all Jesus Christ
On One Leg and It Is Enough

Barbara Smith Sterrett

Everybody Needs Love

I am an American too

I was born September 11th

I have found living in this hard cruel world today has conditioned us to keeping

Everything to our self, even ourselves to ourselves

Let's STOP and recognize

Everybody needs control sometime

And that's alright

But oh when you find you lose control

That's alright sometime

Everybody needs to be alone sometime

And that's alright

But oh when you find you're no longer alone, that's alright sometime

And oh when you find Love's around the corner

That's alright, sometime 'cause

Everybody needs a friend sometime

Everybody needs a friend sometime

Everybody needs a friend sometime

Everybody needs love——————sometime

And that's alright

Barbara Smith Sterrett

Don't Ever Give Up!

When there seems to be no love

Do not give up

When there seem to be no friends

Do not give up

When there seems to be no happiness

Do not give up

When there seems to be no security

Do not give up

When all your friends are gone

Fully rely on God

Think of the frog caught in a bird's throat

Do not give up!

Barbara Smith Sterrett

Chapter VIII

Accolades to Mama on her 90th birthday August 20th, 2019

1 Chronicles 4:10

And Jabez called on the God of Israel: saying, oh thou wouldest bless me indeed, and enlarge my territory, and that thine hand might be with me and thou wouldest keep me from evil that it may not cause me to suffer.

And God granted him that which he requested.

Mama had eight children. The first was raise by her mother. I always say that four of us was raise in sorrow and unhappy circumstances by mama and daddy. 12 years later mama had three more children. I really believe that these three gave her the strength to live and see her VISION.

Mama said she tried to live with other people when daddy was abusive, but it never worked out. She said she prayed to God that he would give her a place of her own. She worked for a white attorney and he helped her to get a house and a acre of land from the government free thirty year later.

I was the 2nd to graduate from high school and the first to graduate from college. Of the first set of children, Larry and Jessie retired from Southeastern in Louisiana on disability. Larry got his GED in Oakland, California and Mama was inspired to get hers and later her Nurses Aide Certificate. She worked at Pike Hospital until she retired. Her last three children: John (Tree) is the pastor of our family church. Lynette retired on disability from the Army and Karen (Neice) got her BA degree in Accounting and works in Baton Rouge, Louisiana where she lives.

Mama has been the Custodian at our home church for over 20 years. When Rev. Primes was the pastor, Mama had a desire to give fruit baskets to the patients at Amite nursing home for Christmas. Mrs. Ruth Curtrer recommenced that the church gives her the funds to do it. The young people and I helped mama to do it.

I was the first Black News Reporter at the News Digest in Amite, owned by Harold Griffin. He sold the paper and is now a pastor of a church. Someone gave mama a poem that is in my book. The poem is called" I'm Determined To Be Somebody Someday". Harold printed it in his paper, and I sent it to friends inJapan and many friends in the United States.

Thank you dear God, for blessing Mama to see her 90th birthday in good health. Thank you for blessing me to surprise her. Please bless her to see, many more birthdays in good health. Amen

Chapter IX

Accolades to Michael Dionn and Bobby Vernell Hooky in from your Mom

1 Chronicles 4:10

Dear Michael and Vernell, this letter are to let you know how grateful and proud I am of you both. You are a blessing to me. I remember when You were very young, I told you that you will be honored someday. I thought that you both would become ministers of the gospel, but God had other plans, which were greater. When you both would turn against each other with kids in the neighborhood I told you both, that you only had each other, so love one another and do not let anyone turn you against each other. Today you are very close, and I am very proud of you both.

Michael you show Leadership around your brother, brothers-laws and your friends, through your words and actions, how to be independent. You have a Poker Club. You showed them how to manage their money, so they learned to travel and take cruises. You encouraged your wife to get her BA degree in Business Administration.

Michael, you and I talk twice a day. If I miss a day calling you, you will say "Mama don't get off your routine ". And you would call me. I love you for that.

Michael, you always looked out for your brother and kepted him on the right path, even when you were a drug dealer. Four years after you gave up selling drugs, your wee shot in your left shoulder by a game member. God spared your life and you exercised your left arm, so you were able to use it. You got your G E D and you worked as a carpenter and for a private company that delivered packages in the Bay Area. You later retired on disability from a back injury.

I remember when we would visit Rev. Carl Hudson and family in Lompoc and later in Milpitas, California and spend the weekend. We also visited many other friends. We would drive to Los Angeles to see Mother Dear. Once we started out and the car broke down in Newman, California and Uncle Larry came and got us. Oftentimes, while traveling, I would get lost, but both of you observed everything and would guide me back to the freeway.

When you both were babies, I would take one of you in my arms and hop around on one leg from room to room. I had a wooden artificial leg and when you wanted my attention, you would knock on my leg and peoples would stare.

I am so grateful that you both are still with your first marriage and didn't make the same mistakes that I did. You couldn't have given me any better Daughter-in-laws.

Vernell, you are a good example for your Daughter, my granddaughter and your friends and co-workers. You sent your daughter to college and with your love, affectionate and actions, you showed her how to be independent.

Her mother had her at age 15 and you were 17, but she was determined not to go down that road. She wasI not like the old saying "like mama, like daughter ". When the parent had babies out of web lock and the children followed and they all were on welfare I am so proud of her. She got her B A degree working with gifted children. She lives in North Hollywood where she finishes college.

Vernell, with the support of your wife and me you

had the courage to go back to college and got your AA and B A degrees. I am very proud of you. You are a Lieutenant in the Oakland Police Department in Oakland, California. You serve as the Chief of Staff for Police Chief Anne Kirkpatrick.You just took your Captain exam and is number 3 on the waiting list. You have been employed for 24 years. You say in two more years you hope to retire..

As your Mom, I like to blow your horn to let others know how proud of you I am. During your career, you worked numerous assignments to include Internal Affairs, the Patrol Division as an Area Commander, Youth and Family Services Division, and S.W.A.T. Team as a Tactical Negotiator.

Some of your accomplishments included receiving a Medal of Merit from the Oakland Police Department and a Meritorious Negotiator Award from the Chief Special Agents' Association of Northern, California, for your success in negotiating peaceful protests in the City of Oakland. Currently you are a lead instructor for Procedural Justice course at the Oakland police Department and the co-founder of the Barbershop Forum.

The Barbershops Forum was founded in July of 2016 by community activist Jack Bryson, Captain Michael Carroll of the Alameda County Sheriff's Office and you. The mission of the Barbershop Forums is to bridge the gap between community and law enforcement via trust, partnership and communication. The Barbershop Forums is designed to connect with impacted communities to build trust on both sides.

I am so proud that you followed the good accomplishments that I did in my life. You are strong and your faith keeps you going.

With your busy schedules, we still talk or text every night. I love you for this. I remember you use to suck your thumb (smile). I am not sure which hand. No matter what I put on your thumb, you still sucked it. I would not allow you on the carpet, so you would stand in the hallway peeking in the living room sucking your thumb. I believe you stopped at the age thirteen.

I can say much more about both of you, but I would like to leave you with these verses from the KJV of the Bible.

Proverbs 33:5-6 Trust in the Lord with all thine heart and lean not unto thine own understanding. In all thy ways acknowledge Him and He shall direct thy path.

Proverbs 4:7 Wisdom is the principal thing, therefore, get wisdom and with all thy getting get understanding.

Love your Mom

12-25-2019

Chapter X
My Move to Livermore, California

I move to Livermore, California November 2016. A person had to be 62 years old to live in the senior complex. I applied for the apartment September 2012. I would call every two months to find out where I was on the list. Management would only say what month and year they were working on and they would say when I get close to the top of the list, they would call me in for recertification. October 16th 2016, they call me and said they had a unit and did I want it? I said "Praise the Lord" I want it. I was on the waiting list four years.

Management found favor in me. I was still following my VISION. I donated my book to the club house library.

As I met new residents and would introduce myself, they would say, I know you Barbara. In 2017, Management ask me to join the Activities Committee. The committee planned functions for the year. I accepted the position. I was the Welcome Person. My responsibility was to send out birthday, get well, sympathy and thinking of you cards ever month.

Once a year the Committee collected a donation of $10.00 from each person to put on the activities for the year. Along with Management, we had a birthday party every quarter. Other activities we put on were: potlucks, Mother Day brunch, Father Day coffee social, Halloween party, Thanksgiving dinner, Christmas Party and New Year Eve party just to name a few.

In November 2019 we had a Veterans Day Event. Sponsor by the Amador Valley Quilts of Valor, the local chapter. The mission of the Quilts of Valor Foundation is to cover Service members and veterans touched by war with comforting and healing Quilts of Valor. We honored seven Veteran's in our community and gave each one a Quilt made and donated by Women of Volour.

We had a community exercise class twice a week before the Pandemic. Now our Service Coordinator has connected our community with a support group that does exercises and meditation once a week.

During the shelter in place, the owners of the complex (SAHA) gave each person in the complex a monetary gift. The Service Coordinator provided games that we could play at home along. He also arranged to have groceries delivered to our door twice a month.

On 4th of July week, Management gave an Ice Cream Social. They brought each unit a cup of ice cream in a gift bag and rang our doorbell. They keep us informed about COVID-19. As of this writing, we are still under "shelter in place".

What Others Had to Say About Barbara (Barbs) in Livermore, California

My name is Jan Higdon. I met Barbara (Babs) in 2008. We went to a Women's Retreat here in Livermore, California together. She was so amazing. For all the hard things she has been through, here was this wonderful Christian Woman praising the LORD and being thankful for her family, friends, the ministry God has given her. She was in 2008 and is still in 2020 so positive. She does have a VISION and she is following it and she has never given up.

My husband and I were able to have her spend a night with us. We had the most wonderful time. I loved her book…We all need a Vision and especially during COVID-19. We need to follow our Vision that the LORD has given us and Never give up.

I read her book. It was amazing. I am so thankful she wrote it. She has had so many hard times in her life, but there she was in January and February of this year greeting people at our church at the front door. We see her Smiling, sharing her faith on Sunday morning in front of a very big class. She is an inspiration to me, my husband, and my daughter who also got to be at the retreat with her in 2008. God is still bringing her through challenges each and evert day. We. Have seem her go from her wheelchair to walking into our church and into our Thursday night bible study with her artificial leg. She has worked so hard to be able to walk again. She had a setback a few years ago having two strokes, but that did NOT stop her from "Following her VISION and NEVER giving up.

Babs inspires our whole church and our whole big Bible class each Thursday night. She is one of the most positive people I have ever met, and I have met some pretty great people in 69 years. BABS is so AMAZING. We all just love her and Thank God daily for her. She is a BLESSING to everyone she meets. I am thankful she wrote her book so people all over the United States and Abroad can meet her and be Blessed by her life and her struggles.

We can all relate to something that she talks about. She has the BEST SMILE and the BEST LAUGH. I enjoy being with her on Sundays and on Thursday nights. I thank God for her everyday and for how God has brought her through so much.

Jan Higdon
Livermore, California
7/13/2020

I am a Rod Davis. Barbara (Babs) has been a friend several years. She is a dedicated Christian who is always thinking of the needs of others.

She knows what her faith in the Lord has done for her and she is all always ready and eager to share Jesus with others. Babs regularly attend worship services-but the thing that stands out is her attendance at our Thursday night Bible Class. Weekly she has to schedule a ride to and from our meeting and pay for them. She is there regularly and participates whole heartedly.

Even though she has gone through many difficult times, she always greets others with a warm smile. Babs is loved by all who know her and her love for a Jesus shows through as she treats others as she wants to be treated. She is a courageous dedicated Christian woman.

Rod Davis
Bible Class Teacher
Livermore, California
7/14/2020

I am Jacob Parnell, preaching minister at Tri Valley Church of Christ in Livermore, California where Babs attends.

Babs enters our church gathering with positivity and warmth. People enjoy seeing Babs and she enjoys seeing them. She's able to have conversations with people of all different age group and backgrounds. Her presence in the worship service contributes to the church's family vibe. I've never seen Babs lose her temper or become irritable with anyone. I've never heard her utter a grumbling, unkind or complaining remark. Her dedication to the Lord is a great example for others in the church.

Jacob Parnell
Preaching Minister
Livermore, California
7/15/2020

Chapter XI

I Tried

I wanted to get out of the wheelchair and walk again. I have been in the wheelchair for 10 years." The stroke left my left leg very weak and later I learn that I have arthritis in my knee, bone on bone. My Doctor said, I am not a good candidate for surgery because I only have one leg. My right arm rotator cuff has a tear in it and arthritis. Surgery was out because I used my arm to lift my body.

Al Higdon, one of the members of my church is a Contractor and he made me an exercises ramp. For a few months I was able to walk with a walker. The pain in my knee and right shoulder began to hurt so bad, my Doctor said I would have to continue to use my wheelchair. Every three months I have to get a cortisone shot in my knee and shoulder for the pain.

I realize that beings in the wheelchair does not stop my VISION. I can still let my light shine wherever I go. Ralph and I went on two cruises to Alaska and I used my electric wheelchair. We went to Louisiana for my mother's 90th birthday and we used the manual wheelchair on the plane. I will never give up

What Others Had to Say

About Barbara Ann Smith-Hookfin-Franklin-Stephen-Sterrett

6-14-2013

I Evelyn Banks from Amite, Louisiana, met Barbara on a three-way telephone conversation with a co-worker. We shared experiences and have confided with each other. I have enjoyed the friendship with Barbara during the short time I've known her. I love Barbara as a third sister of mine.

May God Continue to bless you
Evelyn Banks

3/12/13

My name is Olivia Collier, I am a good friend of Barbara Sterrett. Our friendship has lasted over 30 years.

During these 30 years, Barbara's last name has changed but I have known her to be honest, a businesswoman, a great mother, loving and kind person.

She has always showed great leadership and concern for others.

She is loyal and committed to whomever she devote her time and effort to.

Barbara is the type of person you can admire and get encouragement from. Barbara displays confidence and strength, no matter what the challenge may be. She has weathered the storms of life challenges. She is my hero.

3/10/13

In Regard to My Friend Barbara:

My name is Donna Hall and I am glad to be a sister in Christ to Barbara:
Barbara is my mentor
She gives me inspiration
To be whom I am and never stop
Never doubt, my dreams, hopes
God did it for Barbara and now doing it for me. With his Grace, Mercy and Love
I give thanks to you Father for my friend.

Your Sister-in-Christ
Donna Hall New
Orleans, LA

6-26-2013

I met Barbara in 1965. She was a young and vibrant young Lady so looking forward to getting married, shortly after, she was involved in an accident, which left her handicapped physically, but definitely not mentally. She remained strong.

She did marry and had two sons of which she has always been very proud of and often talked about their accomplishments. She loved them more than my vocabulary can express.

Barbara has always been strong willed and passionate about the things she became involved in – work ethic, friendships, family as well as her Spiritual life. I had the opportunity to meet some of her family members and you could see the love and closeness they shared. She did not mind taking that long drive down here to Los Angeles from Oakland to see them.

Barbara speaks up for the things she believes in and will fight both physically and verbally for them. She founded and managed a handicap center for two years and because of that, many people were encouraged and helped.

She has always professed to love the Lord and her church and even though she has a handicap, she has remained very faithful for many years. She chose not to do as many but has shown that regardless of life's disappointments it is not a reason to stop living but to continue living and make a positive difference in the life of as many as you can.

She is a hard worker and a good person!

From Bettie Hookfin

Los Angeles, CA

3/9/13

My name is Betty Hunter, seeing Barbara through my eyes:

The first thing that comes to mind is her beautiful smile. I first met her at Hurley Creek Senior Apartments where we live, attending a meeting in the clubhouse. I was talking about signing up for Para Transit (disable transportation) and she said "if you need help filling out the form let me know." It seems like if anyone has a problem she will try to help.

She has a great sense of humor, we laugh a lot when we are together. Barbara is a good friend and I'm blessed to have her in my life.

3/8/13

My name is Beth Jenista, I feel so grateful to know you these past 5 years I really enjoyed going to meetings and sitting next to you. You are very quiet, whereas I am loud, so I have to shut up to hear you! You always looked as though you the stuff that I missed. It has been great knowing you, keep in touch.

Beth Jenista

Quincy, IL

3/8/13

My name is Karen Jensen, when I first moved to Hurley Creek Senior Complex January 12, 2102, Barbara was one of the first people I met. She was very friendly and welcomed me with open arms. She has always greeted me with a smile. She is a remarkable, amazing lady and doesn't too many things slow her down. I am very blessed to have gotten to know Barbara.

Hugs

Karen Jensen

Apartment 1314

Sacramento, CA

4/28/13

My name is Glennie Joubert, I've known Barbara Sterrett about 30 years. I first met Barbara at our Bible Study Retreat in Clearlake CA.

I taught Bible study with about 25 women. One of our members brought Barbara to our retreat. I noticed with my physical eyes that she walked with a limp, and later found out that she had a missing limb. But with my spiritual eyes she was free, shouting and praising God.

My first impression of her was, she definitely has a personal relationship with the Lord. She was very independent and positive; always encouraging others. Having Barbara with us and sharing her testimony was one of the most Memorable and Spirit filled classes we've shared.

Throughout the years we have kept in touch, encouraging and praying for each other.

Another occasion I had to share with Barbara was during Hurricane Katrina. I worked with the Red Cross. Barbara called and stated that she and her husband was affected by the hurricane. She continued praising God for sparing her life and blessing her in spite of the circumstances. Barbara and her husband came to my house for clothes and items they could use as a result of the disaster. We prayed and praised God together for His Mercy and Grace throughout the year.

Barbara continues her ministry in the community, helping, encouraging and sacrificing for others, where her light shines bright. Matt: 5:16. Thank you Barbara for being a Blessing in my life, and a constant reminder that Jesus Christ is the same yesterday, today and forever. Heb: 13:8.

God bless you.

Love,

Glennie Joubert

Elk Grove, CA

3/5/13

I Margaret met Barbara in the summer of 2011, when I moved into the nice family orientated complex called Hurley Creek Senior Apartments. She was just sitting in her wheelchair with a beautiful smile. Then she spoke to me and welcomed me to the complex. Before I knew it we were having lunch, hanging out on "The Bench" talking and just enjoying our stay here. As of this day, March 5, 2013, Barbara and I still sit in the sun and enjoy one another's friendship. And if her family love is just as strong I'm sure she's a wonderful mother and successful in her goals. Good luck in everything you aim for.

Margaret Riggins

Sacramento, CA

4/30/13

I Betty Williams first met Barbara Sterrett formally in Clearlake at a women's retreat 30 years ago. In 2005 Barbara was living in Louisiana. We met for lunch at Mike's Cat Fish on Hwy 16 in Amite, LA. We had a wonderful time in fellowship and food.

In 2007, Barbara was a resident at East Louisiana State Hospital in Baton Rouge LA. I visited her as often as I could. We talked about our families and our love for the Lord.

In 2008, Barbara, Mary Kitts and I went to breakfast. Barbara was on her way back to California.

We have remained friends and we talk from Louisiana to California.

In Christ

Betty Williams

Galvez, LA

My Closing Remarks

As I close my book, I thank God that He let me live to have happy relationships and know that I can stand on my own and realize that I am a help mate. I learned that a good marriage takes two people who love and support each other and trust God to direct their path.

Even though I was brought up poor, a divorcee, having one leg, and raising two sons as a single Mom, I was determined to make a difference in the world around me. I was determined that others see me as a strong, confident person. It was important to me to teach my sons to be responsible and dependable young men. I wanted to teach them to respect women and not be verbally or physically abusive.

I was so tired of seeing men being disrespectful and being spoil by their mothers and depending on them. Many of the men that I met were either an alcoholic or on drugs and wanted me to take care of them. As I said earlier in my book, it took 12 mens to make one good one.

I was very stubborn in m young days. I was very impatience when it came to relationships. When I was told I couldn't do something, I would try and do it anyway. I had to have the last word.

I thought that by being a Christian, I should not make mistakes. I didn't want to shack up so that is why I got married. My sons told me later that they wished that I wouldn't have gotten married after Joel. They really liked him. I told them that I thought that they would not respect me if I lived with a man. They said "mom, we will always love you and we realize that you are not perfect."

I regret That the 30 peoples who went to be with the Father in heaven, before they could read my book and see how beautiful I turned out with their love and support. I dedicate my book to them and their families.

There are a few people That I would like to dedicate my book too in Oakland and Hayward, California, Tylertown, Mississippi, Oklahoma City and Pennsylvania that was encouraging to me in my quest.

I wish that the 12 White Jurors, could see that even though they didn't award me any money from the lost of my leg. I still accomplished with the help of God and the people He placed in my path, graduating from college with honors, as well as other achievements.

I realized now that God worked MIRACLES in my life through all my struggles. I'm reminded of David in the Bible, how through his many ups and downs, he cried out to God and God blessed him. A MIRACLE to me is when God does something that I couldn't do for myself.

May my book be encouraging to you as you go through life's struggles. Just remember that Jesus is always near. Amen! Amen! Amen!

About the Author

Barbara Ann Smith-Hookfin-Franklin-Stephen-Sterrett grew up in Smith Hill, 6 miles east of Arcola, Louisiana and 10 miles from Amite City, Louisiana.

She has two sons, their wives, and a granddaughter who live in California.

Her mother, Artis McGowan and her six siblings all live in Louisiana.

She has lived in Tylertown, Mississippi; D'Iberville, Mississippi; Biloxi, Mississippi; Meridian, Mississippi; Marksville, Louisiana; Hammond, Louisiana; Roseland, Louisiana; Los Angeles, California; Lompoc, California; Oakland, California; Dublin, California; Yuba City, California; Sacramento, California and Fayetteville, North Carolina.

She currently lives in a Senior Retirement Community in Livermore, California.

She has visited Fukuoka, Japan in 1981. She was thrilled to go to sing in a concert honoring the international year of the handicap.

Beside having my church home which is located all over the United States and other places for spiritual support, I joined Recovery International, a Suppot Group, they are located across the United States, Canada and other places as well as the United Kingdom. I was an assistant leader in Sacramento, California. When I moved to Livrrmore in the San Francisco Bay Area #20 under David Wister area leader. I started a support group here in Livermore, California.

I was diagnosed with Bipolar disorder, 11 ago, while I was seeing my psychiatrist in Sacramento, my son saw a fler of Recovery International (RI) in the office and told me that it seem interesting and that I should check it out. So, I went.

At the meeting, when I heard examples of things that stress others and the encouragement given them, it encourages me. I never missed a meeting. It was a few months before I starts sharing, but I was learning from the other examples. We called self-help tools SPOTS. The first spot that I used was" Calm begets calm and temper begets temper ".

Once before I went on a cruise, I was nervous, so the spot I used was "nervous symptoms are distressing but not dangerous ". I also learn to say, "have the courage to make a mistake", rather than beat myself up because I made a mistake.

I suffer with fear, so I learn to say, "fear is a belief and beliefs ca be changed". that helped me get rid of some of the negative thoughts that I was having. When I had a lot of things to do, I used the spot, "decide, plan and act". That help me to calm down the racing thoughts and stablize myself.

This is a revision of her life story.

www.ingramcontent.com/pod-product-compliance
Lightning Source LLC
Chambersburg PA
CBHW071509070526
44578CB00001B/486